# EXPLORING THE GREAT LAKES

# PEOPLE
## OF THE GREAT LAKES

U.S. COAST GUARD

47225

Gareth Stevens
PUBLISHING

BY RYAN NAGELHOUT

**Please visit our website, www.garethstevens.com. For a free color catalog of all our high-quality books, call toll free 1-800-542-2595 or fax 1-877-542-2596.**

**Library of Congress Cataloging-in-Publication Data**

Nagelhout, Ryan.
People of the Great Lakes / by Ryan Nagelhout.
p. cm. — (Exploring the Great Lakes)
Includes index.
ISBN 978-1-4824-1206-2 (pbk.)
ISBN 978-1-4824-1192-8 (6-pack)
ISBN 978-1-4824-1432-5 (library binding)
1. Great Lakes (North America) — History — Juvenile literature. 2. Great Lakes Region (North America) — History — Juvenile literature. 3. Indians of North America — Great Lakes (North America) — History — Juvenile literature. I. Nagelhout, Ryan. II. Title.
F551.N34 2015
977—d23

First Edition

Published in 2015 by
**Gareth Stevens Publishing**
111 East 14th Street, Suite 349
New York, NY 10003

Copyright © 2015 Gareth Stevens Publishing

Designer: Michael J. Flynn
Editor: Kristen Rajczak

Photo credits: Cover, pp. 1, 5 courtesy of NOAA; p. 4 courtesy of the US Army Corps of Engineers, Detroit District; p. 7 Underwood Archives/Archive Photos/Getty Images; p. 8 RiverNorthPhotography/Thinkstock.com; p. 10 Hulton Archive/Getty Images; p. 11 Ambroise-Louis Garneray/The Bridgeman Art Library/Getty Images; p. 13 courtesy of NASA; p. 15 http://en.wikipedia.org/wiki/File:WI-Wauwatosa-1892.jpg; pp. 16–17 courtesy of the Library of Congress; p. 18 Bruce MacQueen/Shutterstock.com; p. 19 Gary Blakeley/Shutterstock.com; p. 21 Ira Block/National Geographic/Getty Images; p. 22 SF photo/Getty Images; p. 23 AP Images; p. 24 Scruggelgreen/Shutterstock.com; p. 25 Map Resources/Shutterstock.com; p. 27 jessicakirsh/Shutterstock.com; p. 29 Bustitaway/Thinkstock.com.

Printed in the United States of America

CPSIA compliance information: Batch #CS15GS: For further information contact Gareth Stevens, New York, New York at 1-800-542-2595.

# CONTENTS

Words in the glossary appear in **bold** type
the first time they are used in the text.

# CARVING OUT A HOME

More than 100,000 years ago, a massive glacier called the Laurintide Ice Sheet covered most of North America, from the North Pole to present-day Illinois. Over time, deep grooves were carved into the land. As the planet grew warmer around 14,000 years ago, the ice sheet began to melt, revealing the changed landscape. The grooves slowly filled with water and became the five Great Lakes.

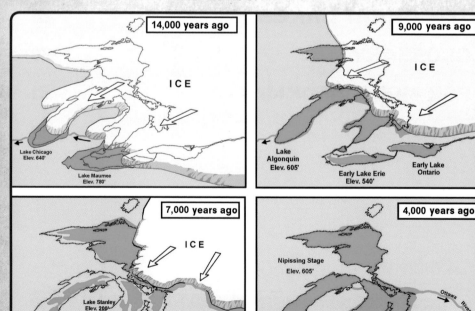

14,000 years ago

ICE

Lake Chicago
Elev. 640'

Lake Maumee
Elev. 780'

9,000 years ago

ICE

Lake
Algonquin
Elev. 605'

Early Lake Erie
Elev. 540'

Early Lake
Ontario

7,000 years ago

ICE

Lake Stanley
Elev. 200'

Lake Chippewa
Elev. 230'

Early Lake Erie
Elev. 540'

Early Lake Ontario

4,000 years ago

Nipissing Stage
Elev. 605'

Ottawa River

St. Lawrence River

Illinois
River

# WHAT ARE THE GREAT LAKES?

The five Great Lakes include Lakes Superior, Huron, Michigan, Erie, and Ontario. Eight states—Illinois, Indiana, Michigan, Minnesota, New York, Ohio, Pennsylvania, and Wisconsin—border the Great Lakes, as does the Canadian **province** of Ontario. The more than 35 million people living in this region rely heavily on the Great Lakes for jobs, transportation, and **natural resources**.

Since the creation of the Great Lakes, millions of people have flocked to their shores. The lakes have shaped the lives of those settling around them. The people of the Great Lakes use the natural resources found there to build a place to call home.

The Great Lakes hold about 20 percent of the world's freshwater.

Lake Superior

Lake Huron

Lake Michigan

Lake Ontario

Lake Erie

# FIRST SETTLERS

About 10,000 years ago, the first inhabitants of the Great Lakes **basin** arrived on the lakes' coasts. The first settlers were ancestors of Native Americans, or First Nations peoples as they're called in Canada.

For thousands of years, they lived off the natural resources of the Great Lakes. They hunted along the lake coasts for food. Copper found south of Lake Superior was used to make weapons and tools. They fished and traveled on the lakes using canoes made from maple and birch trees.

About 120 different tribes have lived around the Great Lakes since the area was first settled.

Native Americans in the Great Lakes region used the lakes for transportation.

# HOW'D THEY GET THERE?

Historians believe the first settlers of the Great Lakes region came to North America from Asia. They may have crossed a land and ice bridge called Beringia (buh-RIHN-jee-uh), which connected present-day Alaska and Russia across what is now the Bering Strait.

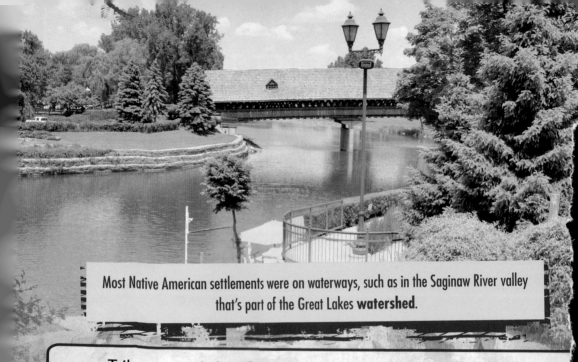

Most Native American settlements were on waterways, such as in the Saginaw River valley that's part of the Great Lakes **watershed**.

Tribes used the Great Lakes basin's fertile land to farm corn, beans, peas, squash, and pumpkins. They would exhaust an area's resources and then move on. Very few permanent settlements were established in the region. Most that existed circled the Great Lakes. Tribes traveled through the forests and plains of the region, but didn't stay long since they needed to stay close to the lakes' resources in order to survive. Between 60,000 and 117,000 Native Americans lived in the Great Lakes region during the 16th century.

The importance of the waterways wasn't lost on the next group of settlers. European explorers began to arrive in the 17th century.

## HOW'D THEY GET THERE?

Historians believe the first settlers of the Great Lakes region came to North America from Asia. They may have crossed a land and ice bridge called Beringia (buh-RIHN-jee-uh), which connected present-day Alaska and Russia across what is now the Bering Strait.

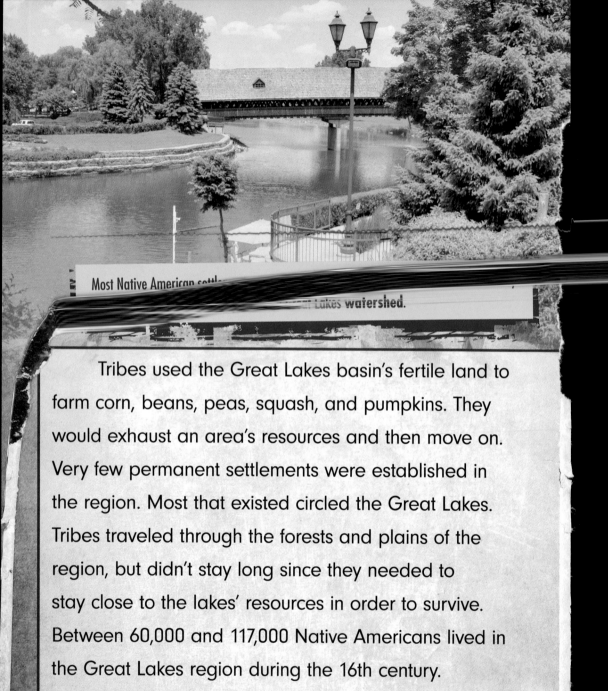

Most Native American settle_____ _____ __ _____ _____ Lakes watershed.

Tribes used the Great Lakes basin's fertile land to farm corn, beans, peas, squash, and pumpkins. They would exhaust an area's resources and then move on. Very few permanent settlements were established in the region. Most that existed circled the Great Lakes. Tribes traveled through the forests and plains of the region, but didn't stay long since they needed to stay close to the lakes' resources in order to survive. Between 60,000 and 117,000 Native Americans lived in the Great Lakes region during the 16th century.

The importance of the waterways wasn't lost on the next group of settlers. European explorers began to arrive in the 17th century.

# FRENCH HERITAGE

The early French settlement of the Great Lakes region influenced it greatly. Today, French is one of the official languages of Canada, along with English. It's the official language of the province of Québec, connected to the Great Lakes region by the St. Lawrence River. Cities in the region bear French names, such as Sault Ste. Marie, Michigan, and Sault Ste. Marie, Ontario, found across from each other on the St. Marys River connecting Lakes Superior and Huron.

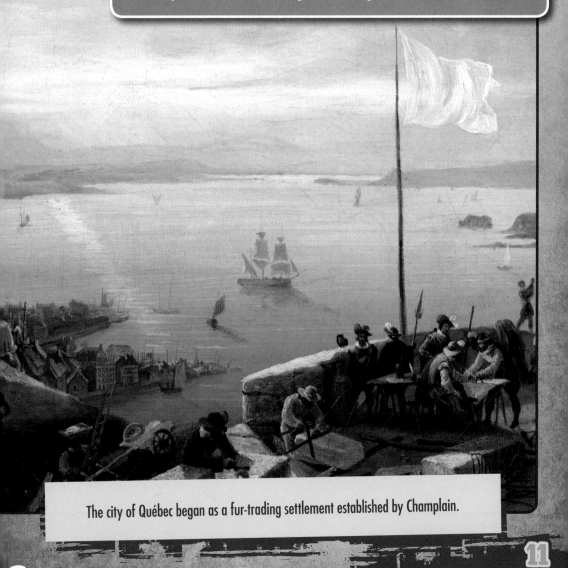

The city of Québec began as a fur-trading settlement established by Champlain.

Over the next century, the fur trade drove settlement in the Great Lakes watershed. Permanent forts began to be built around the lakes. Great Britain began to challenge France's land claims in present-day Canada, and, in 1759, gained control of the region. Then, after the American Revolution ended in 1781, the Great Lakes became part of the border between the United States and British-held Canada.

In 1814, the United States and Great Britain signed the Treaty of Ghent, ending a 2-year conflict now called the War of 1812. It set the course for establishing the current boundary between Canada and the United States and finally allowed US settlers to build up the Great Lakes region as they wanted.

# THE BRITISH INFLUENCE

British control of the Great Lakes region greatly influenced the United States. But Canadians remain tied to Great Britain to this day, even though Canada became an officially independent nation in 1982. The British Queen is also the Queen of Canada, according to a 1953 Canadian law. Elizabeth II doesn't run the country, but she's the head of state, meaning she knows about governmental decisions.

Lake Michigan is the only Great Lake entirely inside the United States. The rest are shared between the United States and Canada. The two countries have many major cities on the five lakes, including Toronto, Ontario, and Chicago, Illinois.

# HOME ON THE LAKES

During the 1800s, people from more than 20 countries came to the Great Lakes. Norwegians founded the first permanent colony on the Fox River in Illinois, while the Swedish settled west of Milwaukee at Pine Lake, Wisconsin. The Irish were the largest **immigrant** group in Canada. People from Finland settled in Michigan and worked copper mines there, while Germans flocked to Sandusky, Ohio, and Milwaukee.

These immigrants farmed along the lakes' shores. The fur trade continued through the early 1800s, but as more settlers came, it moved westward. The Native Americans they traded with were also pushed west as cities began to grow around the Great Lakes.

# NATIVE AMERICANS TODAY

Though many Native Americans were pushed west as settlement increased, their cultures left their mark, including in names of cities and waterways, such as Wisconsin's Menomonee Falls. Some tribes are still present in the region today. They celebrate their history by creating art and music. Many are involved in natural-resource protection, too. The Keweenaw Bay Indian Community in Michigan, for example, is working with the US Fish and Wildlife Service to restore the lake trout population in the Great Lakes.

Milwaukee is the largest city in Wisconsin. It grew on Lake Michigan during the 1800s after an agreement with local Native American tribes opened the area to settlers.

Those living around the Great Lakes used the available natural resources to start profitable industries. They used the lakes and built canals for shipping. The logging industry grew because of the great forests near the lakes.

By the mid-1800s, farmers around the Great Lakes were harvesting wheat and corn, packing their crops in barrels, and shipping them across the country. Grist mills where these grains were ground grew up around the Great Lakes region. Dairy and meat farms fed the growing local population, and fruit, vegetables, and tobacco were also grown around the lakes.

Logging began in the thick forests of the lakes, first in Canada, and a few years later in Michigan, Minnesota, and Wisconsin. These logging operations produced lumber and used lake water and wood for making paper. The logging companies and nearby paper mills attracted workers, too.

# INDUSTRY ISN'T EVERYTHING

While the Great Lakes region became a profitable center of logging and paper production, these industries caused problems, too. Companies cutting down too many trees destroyed the homes of many animals and plants. Early papermaking practices polluted the Great Lakes with a chemical called mercury, a problem that continued until the 1970s, when using mercury to make paper was banned.

Detroit loggers in the 1800s, like those shown here, cut down forests of white pine to be made into wagons, ships, and furniture.

# BIG CITIES

Other Great Lakes industries became essential to the American economy as the 20th century began. For the first half of the 1900s, Chicago was a center of the meatpacking industry. The auto industry blossomed in Detroit, and cars and trucks built there were shipped around the world. Buffalo, New York, became a major center for the steel and grain industries. Big grain silos lined some of the city's Lake Erie shores.

The jobs created by these growing industries attracted many people. Chicago doubled its population between 1880 and 1890 to more than 1 million people, and doubled it again to 2.2 million by 1910.

grain silos

# THE GREAT MIGRATION

From 1916 to 1970, 6 million African Americans moved north and west from the southern United States in what was called the "Great Migration." They flocked to the Great Lakes region in search of better work opportunities and improved **civil rights**. Many settled in cities like Chicago and Detroit, especially during World War I and World War II. They often worked in factories, but the jobs they were given were often dangerous.

Toronto, Ontario, grew greatly in the second half of the 20th century. Today, it produces more than half of the manufactured goods in Canada and is a transportation center of trucking, rail, and shipping by water.

Read some fun facts about some of the major Great Lakes cities!

▷ More than 20 percent of Illinois's population lives in Chicago.

▷ The total land area of Toronto is 2,280 square miles (5,906 sq km). There are almost 2,450 people living in each square mile (2.6 sq km)!

▷ As of 2012, Duluth, Minnesota, had a population of 86,211. However, more than 3.5 million people visit the city each year!

▷ Great Lakes residents know winter well. Buffalo and Rochester, New York; Erie, Pennsylvania; and Duluth have some of the highest snowfall totals in the country.

## CROSSING THE BORDER

To cross the US-Canadian border, you must present certain kinds of identification, such as a passport. This is the law for all those traveling between the countries by car or plane, or by boat across the Great Lakes. Many places along the Great Lakes are official ports of entry to Canada or the United States. The Peace Bridge, which connects Buffalo, New York, and Fort Erie, Ontario, is named for a fact both nations are proud of: the United States and Canada have the longest peaceful border in the world.

In 1977, a huge snowstorm hit Buffalo, New York. Cars were buried in snow, and people were stranded at schools and businesses. The National Guard had to come help dig the city out!

# MAKING CONNECTIONS

People living on the Great Lakes have changed the lakes so their resources can be better used. The Welland Canal in Ontario, for example, connects Lake Ontario to Lake Erie. It was built so that large ships could move between the two lakes and bypass Niagara Falls.

The Soo **Locks** on the St. Marys River in Michigan allow ships to sail around the river's rapids. St. Marys River is the only connection between Lake Superior and Lake Huron, and the set of four locks makes the 21-foot (6.4 m) drop from the levels of Lake Superior to Lake Huron possible for travel.

Welland Canal

# THE ERIE CANAL

In 1825, the opening of the 363-mile (584 km) Erie Canal aided travel and shipping throughout the Great Lakes region. It created a path for boat traffic to travel east to the Hudson River, which led to New York City and the Atlantic Ocean.

The Soo Locks are found in Sault Ste. Marie, Michigan. A fur company built the first lock there in 1797 on the Canadian side, but it was destroyed in the War of 1812.

The completion of the Erie Canal in 1825 made it easier to transport people and goods to and from the Great Lakes region. Today, millions of dollars of iron ore, coal, grains, and limestone are shipped through the Great Lakes waterways. The Detroit River, which connects Lake Erie to Lake St. Clair, is one such waterway.

Duluth, Minnesota, has the largest port on the Great Lakes, found on the western tip of Lake Superior. It's also the westernmost point on the St. Lawrence Seaway, which is made up of a series of man-made locks and canals that connected the Great Lakes to the Atlantic Ocean in 1959.

Duluth, Minnesota

# St. Lawrence Seaway

Lake Superior

Mackinac Bridge

St. Lawrence River

Lake Huron

Duluth, Minnesota

Lake Ontario

Lake St. Clair

Detroit River

Lake Erie

Lake Michigan

Atlantic Ocean

The term "St. Lawrence Seaway" often refers to all the navigable waterways in the Great Lakes region, including the St. Lawrence River. The official seaway connects Duluth to the head of the St. Lawrence, more than 2,000 miles (3,219 km) away.

# MIGHTY MAC

The Mackinac (MAA-kuh-naw) Bridge is an important transportation route in Michigan. The 5-mile (8 km) span is the longest **suspension bridge** in the Western Hemisphere, crossing the Straits of Mackinac where Lake Michigan and Lake Huron meet. When construction finished in 1957, the "Mighty Mac" bridge turned a 1-hour ferry ride across the water into an easy car ride, better allowing people to travel around and through the state.

# THE CHANGING ECONOMY

The population centers around the Great Lakes exploded during the late 1800s and early 1900s, but recent years have seen big changes in Great Lakes cities. Steel production shifted overseas in the 1970s and 1980s, and major factories have closed because of it. The shifting American economy means the people of the Great Lakes are changing, too.

Chicago and Toronto have become centers for commerce, headquarters of major companies, and remain transportation centers. Other cities, such as Detroit, deal with the loss of industry and try to reinvent themselves as their people move to other areas of the country.

# POPULATION LOSS

Detroit has lost more than 25 percent of its population over the last decade. It's one of many Rust Belt cities. Cities in the Great Lakes region that lost major industries during the second half of the 20th century are considered part of the Rust Belt, since one of the key industries lost was steel, which rusts when neglected. The Rust Belt commonly includes places like Pittsburgh, Pennsylvania, as well as many Great Lakes cities such as Buffalo, New York, and Cleveland, Ohio.

The population of different cities often changes based on the availability of jobs.

# THE GREAT LAKES TODAY

About 10 percent of the United States' and 31 percent of Canada's population live in the Great Lakes basin. That doesn't include visitors! Tourism is a big industry in the Great Lakes, one that brings people to beautiful beaches, nature reserves, and bustling cities year-round. Sport fishing, sailing, and other water activities are popular, as are birding and skiing.

From furs to steel to today's often-shifting economy, the people of the Great Lakes have learned to adapt to whatever comes their way. One thing doesn't change for the people of this region, however: their ability to rely on the great natural resources of the Great Lakes.

# GREAT LAKES POPULATION CHART

Here are the 10 most populated cities and their **metropolitan areas** in the Great Lakes region. Canadian city populations are from 2011, and US city populations are from 2012.

| city | state/ province | lake(s) | city population | metro population |
|------|-----------------|---------|-----------------|------------------|
| Chicago | Illinois | Michigan | 2.7 million | 9.52 million |
| Toronto | Ontario | Ontario | 2.6 million | 5.6 million |
| Detroit | Michigan | Michigan | 701,475 | 4.3 million |
| Cleveland | Ohio | Erie | 390,928 | 2 million |
| Milwaukee | Wisconsin | Michigan | 598,916 | 1.6 million |
| Buffalo | New York | Erie/Ontario | 259,384 | 1.1 million |
| Rochester | New York | Ontario | 210,532 | 1 million |
| Hamilton | Ontario | Ontario | 519,949 | 721,053 |
| Syracuse | New York | Ontario | 144,170 | 660,934 |
| Toledo | Ohio | Erie | 284,012 | 608,711 |

Visitors to the Great Lakes region can enjoy both city life and nature.

# GLOSSARY

**basin:** the land drained by a body or bodies of water

**civil rights:** the personal freedoms granted to US citizens by law

**immigrant:** a person who comes to a new country to live there

**lock:** a closed area in a canal used in raising or lowering boats as they pass from one water level to another

**metropolitan area:** a major city and the suburbs and towns around it

**natural resource:** a place or thing that provides something useful

**province:** a political unit of a country

**suspension bridge:** a bridge with a road held by two or more cables usually passing over towers and strongly anchored at the ends

**watershed:** an area of land whose water drains into a particular river or waterway

# FOR MORE INFORMATION

## BOOKS

Kummer, Patricia K. *The Great Lakes.* New York, NY: Marshall Cavendish Benchmark, 2009.

Piehl, Janet. *The Great Lakes.* Minneapolis, MN: Lerner Publications, 2010.

Sjonger, Rebecca, and Bobbie Kalman. *Nations of the Eastern Great Lakes.* New York, NY: Crabtree Publishing, 2005.

## WEBSITES

**Great Lakes Quiz**
*dnr.wi.gov/org/caer/ce/eek/cool/GreatLakesQuiz/*
See how much you know about the Great Lakes with this fun quiz.

**Indians of the Midwest**
*publications.newberry.org/indiansofthemidwest/wp-content/ themes/plainscape/maps/map2/*
Explore the early forts and tribes on the Great Lakes with this interactive map.

**2010 US Population Map**
*census.gov/2010census/popmap/*
Find out where some of the biggest cities in the country are with this interactive census map.

# INDEX